AF096372

RODRI

RODRI

ODYSSEYS

AIDAN WHITCOMB

CREATIVE EDUCATION · CREATIVE PAPERBACKS

Published by Creative Education and Creative Paperbacks
P.O. Box 227, Mankato, Minnesota 56002
Creative Education and Creative Paperbacks are imprints
of The Creative Company
www.thecreativecompany.us

Design and production by Blue Design, Inc. (www.bluedes.com)
Art direction by Tom Morgan

Images by Associated Press/Jose Breton, cover; Dreamstime/Chiraphat Phaungmala, 28, Oleksandr Prykhodko, 72; Getty Images/Alex Gottschalk/DeFodi Images, 51, Alex Grimm, 35, ANDER GILLENEA, 24, Aurelien Meunier - PSG, 46, Francois Nel - UEFA, 2, GABRIEL BOUYS, 52, GIUSEPPE CACACE, 68, Jan Kruger - UEFA, 67, JAVIER SORIANO, 60, John Walton - EMPICS , 16, JOSE JORDAN, 19, LINDSEY PARNABY, 45, Matteo Ciambelli/DeFodi Images, 56, Michael Regan - FIFA, 59, Michael Regan - UEFA, 75, Mike Egerton - PA Images, 42, NurPhoto, 4-5, 11, OLI SCARFF , 64-65, Simon Stacpoole/Offside, 8, STRINGER, 20; Unsplash/Florian Wehde, 12; Wikimedia Commons/Poetisasum, 26, Rolandhino1, 6

Every effort has been made to contact copyright holders for material reproduced in this book. Any omissions will be rectified in subsequent printings if notice is given to the publisher.

Copyright © 2026 Creative Education, Creative Paperbacks
International copyright reserved in all countries. No part of this book may be reproduced in any form without written permission from the publisher.

Library of Congress Cataloging-in-Publication Data
Names: Whitcomb, Aidan author
Title: Rodri / By Aidan Whitcomb.
Description: Mankato, Minnesota : Creative Education and Creative Paperbacks, [2026] | Series: Odysseys in sports: soccer stars | Includes bibliographical references and index. | Audience: Ages 12-15 | Audience: Grades 7-9 | Summary: "Instrumental in both Manchester City's historic treble and Spain's Euro 2024 wins, defensive midfielder Rodri won the 2024 Ballon d'Or. Soar along with the Spanish star in this action-packed biography for early high school readers"– Provided by publisher.
Identifiers: LCCN 2025012527 (print) | LCCN 2025012528 (ebook) | ISBN 9798895811429 library binding | ISBN 9798896800958 paperback | ISBN 9798895812686 ebook
Subjects: LCSH: Hernández Cascante, Rodrigo, 1996–Juvenile literature | Soccer players-Spain-Biography-Juvenile literature | Soccer midfielders-Spain-Biography-Juvenile literature | Manchester City Football Club-Juvenile literature
Classification: LCC GV942.7.H444 W46 2026 (print) | LCC GV942.7.H444 (ebook) | DDC 796.334092 [B]-dc23/eng/20250606
LC record available at https://lccn.loc.gov/2025012527
LC ebook record available at https://lccn.loc.gov/2025012528

Printed in the United States

CONTENTS

Introduction 9

A Rocky Start 13

International Duty 20

School/Soccer Balance 26

An Upward Trajectory 29

Sharing the Field with Idols 35

Champions League Debut 39

Welcome to Manchester 40

Scoring in the Premier League 45

Crushing Champions League Exit 52

Atop the Soccer World 57

Best Club 68

Euros Glory 75

Selected Bibliography 76

Glossary 77

Websites 79

Index 80

Introduction

It's the 68th minute of the 2023 **UEFA Champions League** (UCL) final. Manchester City and Inter Milan are locked in a 0–0 stalemate at Istanbul's Atatürk Olympic Stadium. City have been on the front foot but are still searching for the breakthrough. Suddenly, Bernardo Silva latches onto a through ball, sprints into the box, and attempts to cut a pass back across the endline. The pass is

OPPOSITE: Rodri celebrates his goal during the 2023 UEFA Champions League final between Manchester City and Inter Milan.

deflected off a Milan defender and rolls to the edge of the area, where Rodri arrives in stride. With perfect precision, he unleashes a curled strike through a crowd of black and blue shirts, and into the net. Rodri celebrates as the Manchester fans erupt, their first Champions League title in reach.

Typically, the attack-minded soccer players receive the most recognition. The forwards known for their eye for the goal or flashy dribbling ability are the superstars. But often, a team's success is dependent on players who do the dirty work; players who can make a tackle, pass cleanly, and be consistent. These unsung heroes—like the lanky Spanish boy who went from being cut by his youth team to atop the soccer world—deserve a platform to shine, too.

Rodri demonstrates exceptional ball control.

A Rocky Start

Rodrigo Hernández Cascante was born June 22, 1996, in Madrid, Spain. Growing up in a soccer-crazed city, Rodri naturally grew to love the game. His family was supportive of his soccer dreams but also emphasized the value of discipline and education. His first club was Villanueva de la Cañada in a tiny town just outside Madrid. After that, he played for Rayo Majadahonda. From a young age, he began to develop as a defensive midfielder,

OPPOSITE: Rodri was born and grew up in the Spanish capital, Madrid.

a position often neglected at the youth levels. Rodri naturally admired other Spanish defensive midfielders, like Xabi Alonso and Sergio Busquets. Rodri's intelligence and composure—key traits for that position—stood out to coaches.

When he was just 11 years old, Rodri joined the Atlético Madrid youth academy, Atlético Infantil. While in the academy, Rodri held to his family's advice and remained committed to his schooling. Rodri's talent was clear to coaches. His vision and soccer IQ stood out. The academy helped develop his all-around defensive skills. Rodri also improved his passing precision. He had impressive range for a prospect and could launch a counterattack from anywhere. Teammates respected Rodri's calmness and maturity. Rodri even got the opportunity to represent Spain twice at the U16 level in 2012.

There were also some concerns. As a teen, Rodri was smaller than many of his peers. Some believed he wasn't strong enough to play defensive midfield. Coaches experimented with his positioning, trying to find him a spot on the field. Though he was one of the hardest workers in the academy, the coaches felt Rodri wouldn't be a fit with the first team. In 2013, Atlético made the difficult decision to release Rodri, citing concerns about his physical development. For many, being released as

Rodri overcame physical limitations as a youth to shine in defensive midfield.

a 17-year-old could be career ending. Some find new clubs to bounce back, but others don't. While Rodri was extremely disappointed, he knew he couldn't give up, and he used his release as motivation into the next stages of his career.

Soon after his departure from Atlético, Villarreal scooped him up. They saw something in Rodri that Atlético didn't. Ignoring his physical limitations at 19, Villarreal took a chance on him. They believed he had the work ethic and intelligence to blossom into a star. Villarreal is highly respected in Spain for their youth scouting networks and their academy coaches. In the Villarreal youth system, Rodri progressed both in technical ability and physicality. In the 2014–15 season, 18-year-old Rodri competed with the Villarreal Juvenil A team in the División de Honor Juvenil de Fútbol. In 30 matches, Rodri helped guide Villarreal to a top-of-the-league finish in the division's Group VII. They edged out the Valencia youth team by one point, qualifying for the Copa de Campeones.

The 2014–15 edition of the Copa de Campeones was filled with eight of Spain's most notable youth teams. A 3–1 win over Real Sociedad in the quarterfinals and a 1–0 victory over Rayo Vallecano in the semifinals set up Rodri and Villarreal with a chance to win their first Copa de Campeones trophy. The game was a rematch of the 2008 final where Espanyol won a tight 2–1 affair. Villarreal took a quick 2–0 lead, but a pair of late Espanyol goals sent the game to extra time. In extra time, Villarreal right back Genís received a second yellow card. His team looked vulnerable, but Rodri pulled it together and calmed the game down. Just six minutes later, Villarreal's

Rodri was key to Villarreal Juvenil's success.

International Duty

Following the 2014-15 season, Rodri was selected for the UEFA European Under-19 Championship (U19 **Euros**). Rodri was a staple in the Spanish lineup. A win, draw, and loss were enough for Spain to advance out of the group and into the semifinals. Spain squeaked by France 2-0 and advanced into the final. France's team included Rodri's friend Lucas Hernandez, from his time with Atlético Madrid's youth team. In the final, Spain defeated Russia 2-0, claiming their record 10th title. Rodri was selected in the Team of the Tournament. He was a blossoming star in Spain's youth setup, setting the foundation for his future in the national team.

Mathías Rodríguez scored a late winner. Rodri helped the team across the finish line, as Villarreal Juvenil won their first Copa de Campeones title.

Throughout the youth league season, Rodri also was called up for a handful of appearances with the Villarreal B senior team. Villarreal B is a reserve team that competed in the Segunda División B, the third level of Spanish soccer. Rodri made his senior **debut** for the reserves on February 7, 2015, as a substitute against Espanyol B. He made his first start two weeks later in a 2–0 win over

Real Zaragoza B. Over the course of the season, Rodri made seven reserve team appearances. In the summer, Rodri earned a call up to the U19 national team for the U19 Euros, where he helped Spain win the tournament. Rodri's performances caught the eyes of scouts around Europe, as well as coaches in the senior national team.

The 2015–16 season was Rodri's breakout year. Villarreal began to phase Rodri out of the Juvenil team and fully into the reserves team. He began as a starter for Villarreal B, kicking the season off with a 3–1 victory over L'Hospitalet. Rodri enjoyed personal and team success throughout the course of the Segunda División B season. Manager Paco López leaned on Rodri as a stabilizing player, and it became almost impossible to exclude the 19-year-old. Rodri's consistency caught the eye of first-team manager Marcelino who wished to reward the player with a debut. After suffering the disappointment of being released from Atlético Madrid, Rodri had completely revitalized his career and now got his first chance with the first team.

On December 17, 2015, Rodri debuted for Villarreal's first team in the second **leg** of a Copa del Rey round-of-32 match against Huesca. Rodri controlled the midfield, and his wide ball to Denis Suárez was integral in the buildup for Villarreal's second goal.

Rodri gets instructions from Villarreal manager Marcelino.

Rodri made two more appearances before returning to the reserves, where he continued his solid year. He turned in great performances throughout the spring.

As Rodri continued to impress Marcelino, the manager called Rodri up for a La Liga match against Rayo Vallecano. On April 17, 2016, Rodri made his La Liga debut, coming in as a 71st-minute substitute for Suárez. Three days later, Rodri featured in La Liga against the giants of world soccer, Real Madrid, at the Estadio Bernabéu. On April 24, Rodri scored his first goal for the Villarreal B team. In a scrappy goal that represented just the kind of player he is, Rodri scored from a seated position after being tackled just in front of the net. Rodri outmuscled his defender from the ground and slid it past the goalkeeper. It put a cap on a week of

School/Soccer Balance

During his time as a Villarreal youth player, Rodri was also studying at Jaume I University. Rodri wished to honor his family's educational values. Very few professional players went to university while pursuing their sporting career, so balancing his schooling and soccer was difficult. Some days Rodri had to hustle between class and training with his club, which made for a unique experience. While at university, Rodri worked toward a degree, which he would eventually finish years later, in business administration and management. It would have been a difficult task for many—but not for the extremely disciplined and intelligent Rodri.

career moments for Rodri. A week later, he made his first career La Liga start in a 2–0 win over Valencia.

Villarreal B also had a great year as they finished second in the Group 3 league table, winning 20 of their 38 matches. This finish qualified them for the promotion playoffs. In his final actions as a reserve player, Rodri tried to will his team into the Segunda División. Unfortunately, Rodri and the team were bounced in the first round. Rodri did score an equalizing goal in the second leg, but the team was eliminated on the away goals tiebreaker. Still, Rodri had broken into the first team and was on a great career trajectory as a young player. Training alongside veteran pros helped Rodri see what he needed to have a long career in top leagues. He was truly a gifted youngster whose calmness, passing, and tackling impressed everyone.

An Upward Trajectory

Rodri transitioned from promising youngster to key member of the first team across the 2016–17 season. However, Rodri did not start the year as an everyday player. Just days before the start of the season, manager Marcelino left Villarreal. New manager Fran Escribá took over the reins and tended to lean on his experienced core to start the year.

OPPOSITE: Rodri played for Villarreal until rejoining Atlético Madrid in 2018–19.

Rodri got his first taste of action on Matchweek 8 of the La Liga campaign, coming in as an 81st-minute sub in a 5–0 thrashing of Celta Vigo. A few weeks later, Rodri made his European debut in the 2016–17 UEFA [Europa League]{.orange} as he was given a start against Turkish club Osmanlıspor. Rodri scored his first European goal early in the second half. It wasn't the prettiest goal, but a massive deflection off his defender looped the ball over the wrong-footed goalie.

As the season progressed, Rodri saw an increased workload, making starts or substitute appearances in nearly every match. In a 3–1 victory against Sporting Gijón in April, Rodri recorded his first La Liga assist. In total, Rodri helped Villarreal to an up-and-down season across all competitions. While Rodri's impact didn't necessarily show up on the scoresheet, he certainly made positive contributions with his positional discipline and control. The 20-year-old controlled the tempo of a match better than many players his senior. He finished the season with 31 total appearances. Larger clubs around Spain began adding Rodri to their wish list, but for the moment, Rodri seemed committed to Villarreal.

In the summer, Rodri was selected to compete in the 2017 UEFA European Under-21 Championship. Rodri played sparingly, with his only appearance coming in the final group stage game against Serbia, where he played the full match in a 1–0 victory. Spain made it all the way to the final against Germany, but Rodri watched from the sidelines as Spain lost 0–1. Still, his national team opportunities continued into the next season, as he started in numerous U21 Euros qualifiers.

In Rodri's breakthrough 2017–18 season, he became an everyday starter at 21 years old. However, Villarreal started shakily. After six matches, Villarreal sat in 14th place in the league. Escribá got the boot after just more than a year. The club chose to go with Javier Calleja, the team's youth coach, as the new manager. This time, the transition was much smoother for Rodri, as he became one of Calleja's favorites. Rodri helped steady the Villarreal ship after the slow start. Clubs around Europe upped their interest in the blossoming star. People compared him to a young Sergio Busquets, citing their work on both sides of the field and great passing vision. On December 4, Rodri renewed his contract with Villarreal, signing a deal extending into 2022. The extension also raised his release fee, increasing the potential future profit if the club chose to let Rodri leave.

Rodri scored his first La Liga goal on February 18, 2018, in a 1–1 draw at Espanyol. Rodri collected the ball off a blocked Enes Ünal shot and blasted it past the keeper. Throughout the La Liga season, Rodri also added three assists. In all competitions with Villarreal, Rodri led the team with 47 appearances and became one of the top midfield prospects in all of Spain. Transfer rumors continued to swirl. He also led La Liga in ball recoveries and had the third most successful passes. Rodri helped Villarreal to a fifth-place finish, rebounding from the poor start. For his efforts, Rodri received his first call-up to the senior national team, debuting in March 2018. It was another proud moment for Rodri and his family.

Following the season, Rodri's future changed significantly when Spanish giant Atlético Madrid reached an agreement with Villarreal for his transfer. The team

Sharing the Field with Idols

In March 2018, Rodri received the call from Spanish manager Julen Lopetegui selecting him for two friendlies against 2014 **FIFA** World Cup finalists Germany and Argentina. On March 23, Lopetegui handed the 21-year-old his international debut, subbing him on for Thiago Alcántara in the 82nd minute. Rodri shared the field with Spanish soccer royalty: Andres Iniesta, Gerard Piqué, and Sergio Ramos, all players he had watched win the World Cup eight years before. Off the back of his debut, Rodri maybe would have thought he'd sneak onto the 23-man World Cup squad. Unfortunately, he was passed over for more experienced defensive midfielders like Busquets and Thiago.

that released him just a few seasons prior realized the mistake. On May 24, Rodri signed a five-year contract with the club for around $23.5 million.

Rodri's first action for his new team came in a preseason **friendly** against Arsenal in Singapore. The game went to penalty kicks where Rodri converted in a victory. Rodri made his competitive debut immediately after in the 2018 UEFA **Super Cup**. Manager Diego Simeone put a lot of faith into his summer signing, starting him in the team's opener. The match was a Madrid **derby** in Tallinn, Estonia. Rodri played the opening 71 minutes. The game ended in a thrilling 4–2 victory over Real for Atlético after extra time.

Rodri was integral to Simeone's setup. Known for being a defense-minded manager, Simeone used Rodri to perfection, relying on his ability to cover ground and passing. Rodri's performance at an elite club solidified him as one of the best midfielders in Europe. He also broke into the Spanish national team under new manager Luis Enrique. On September 11, 2018, Rodri appeared in his first competitive match for Spain, playing the final 32 minutes of a 6–0 smashing of Croatia in the UEFA **Nations League**.

In La Liga, Rodri made 34 appearances with 32 starts. Rodri's first goal for his new club came in a November La Liga match against Athletic Club. With his team down 1–2 in the 80th-minute, Rodri elevated highest off a Thomas Partey corner kick, heading the ball into the net, leveling the match. Goals against Alavés and a sensational left-footed rocket on the final day against Levante brought his league total to three. With Rodri pulling the strings, Atlético Madrid had their best La Liga finish since their 2013–14 title, finishing as runners-up to Barcelona. Rodri also made his debut in the Champions League, making eight appearances.

Once more, Rodri received interest from teams across Europe. His comparisons to Busquets increased. Every team around the world was desperate to get their hands on the type of player Rodri was. A defensive anchor with an exceptional pass completion rate is exactly what possession-dominant teams craved. Two teams seemed most keen to get Rodri, Bayern Munich and Manchester City. Both had aging defensive midfielders nearing the

Champions League Debut

The 2018-19 season was Rodri's first chance to play in the Champions League. Rodri appeared in all eight of Atlético Madrid's matches, contributing to the team's stellar defense, who kept clean sheets in their last three group games. Atlético Madrid advanced out of the group tied with Borussia Dortmund and were matched against Cristiano Ronaldo's Juventus in the round of 16. After a brilliant 2-0 home win in the first leg, things were looking good for Rodri to advance into the quarterfinals. However, Ronaldo showed his greatness in the second leg, scoring a hat trick to lead the Italian side past Atlético.

end of their elite playing days. Each informed Rodri of their desire to purchase him, but the chance to work under fellow Spaniard Pep Guardiola in Manchester was too much for Bayern to compete with in the end.

On July 3, 2019, Manchester City activated Rodri's $79 million release clause and brought him to England. The signing was the most expensive in club history. Rodri raved about City after the news broke, complimenting the talented squad, style of soccer, and everything the club had achieved in the past couple of seasons.

RODRI

Welcome to Manchester

In his first season with Manchester City, Rodri played an essential role in the midfield. Under Guardiola, Rodri vastly improved. He was plugged into the starting lineup immediately, debuting in the **FA Community Shield** against Liverpool on August 4, 2019. City won on penalty kicks, as Rodri lifted a trophy in his first game. He made his English **Premier League** (EPL) debut six days later in a 5–0 win against West Ham and scored his first goal a few weeks into the year at Norwich. Rodri also began to be a regular with the Spanish national team, making numerous appearances in UEFA Euro 2020 qualifiers.

City's best competition of the season was the **EFL Cup**. The team made easy work of the opening rounds, to set up a pair of semifinals derbies against Manchester United. A 3–2 aggregate win sent City into the final against Aston Villa. With Liverpool pulling away in the EPL, City and Rodri were desperate to add a trophy to the season's haul. In the final, Rodri delivered. He started the move for the City opener and scored the second on a header from a perfect Ilkay Gündoğan corner. City won 2–1, claiming their seventh EFL Cup title.

City's 2019–20 UCL experience was a mixed bag. After an unbeaten group phase, many considered the team as real contenders. But the COVID-19 pandemic interrupted the tournament, and the run ended in the quarterfinals, as Lyon shocked the favorites in a 3–1 upset.

OPPOSITE Rodri (third from left, wearing a jersey with his full name) scores for Manchester City.

Rodri, subbed earlier in the match for an attack option, watched from the bench as his team was eliminated. While City weren't able to win a third consecutive EPL title or their first UCL, Rodri still walked away with a pair of trophies. He also scored a career high four goals and added a pair of assists.

City rebounded in the 2020–21 season, and Rodri was a crucial fixture in Guardiola's squad. Rodri improved upon his already spectacular passing accuracy and his ball-winning skills for the Premier League's best defensive side. In the league, Rodri made 34 appearances, scoring and assisting twice, finishing second in completed passes. He was especially proficient with his long passing stats, finishing second in completion percentage at 85 percent. City ran away as champions, finishing 12 points ahead of Manchester United. Another EFL Cup win added to

Rodri's quickly growing trophy cabinet. He also scored his first career goal for Spain in a Nations League group game against Germany.

The UCL was the only competition Guardiola had failed to win since arriving in Manchester. Belief was at an all-time high, as City coasted through their group opponents. Things started well for City in the knockouts where Rodri's defensive effort helped City ease past Borussia Mönchengladbach with a pair of 2–0 shutouts. In two quarterfinal matches against Borussia Dortmund, City came out on top with a pair of 2–1 victories. Rodri dealt with Paris Saint-Germain's high-octane attack in the semifinals. In the first leg, Rodri shut down Neymar and Kylian Mbappé en route to a 2–1 win. In the second leg, Guardiola opted for the veteran Fernandinho instead of Rodri. City won 2–0, confirming their spot

Scoring in the Premier League

Rodri scored his first Premier League goal in a wild match against newly promoted Norwich City. The defending champions were heavy favorites, but two quick Norwich goals shocked City and another just after halftime made it 1-3. Needing a spark, the unlikely Rodri came through. Receiving the ball from Gabriel Jesus at the top of the box, Rodri unleashed a low laser past the outstretched Tim Krul in the 88th minute. Rodri continued to push City forward through the game's closing moments, but City were denied a victory. It was a day of mixed emotions for Rodri.

Rodri in a one-on-one battle with another great, Neymar

in the final, as Rodri did not feature. Few questioned Guardiola's decision, but who would start in the final against Chelsea remained unanswered.

On May 29, Guardiola named his 11 for the biggest match in team history. Rodri was not in the starting lineup. Neither was Fernandinho. Instead, the manager played Gündoğan out of position in the central defensive midfielder (CDM) role. In the match, City struggled to gain a foothold in the midfield. In the 35th minute, Gündoğan picked up a yellow card, and in the 42nd minute, Kai Havertz scored for Chelsea. Rodri watched on in frustration. In the second half, Guardiola opted for Fernandinho ahead of Rodri. City failed to score, losing 1–0. The system responsible for their dominant campaign was inexplicably thrown out. It was only the second match of the season that neither Rodri nor

Fernandinho started. The snubbing left a sour taste in Rodri's mouth, and he was determined to make amends the next season.

Over the summer, Rodri represented Spain at the postponed UEFA Euro 2020. With captain Busquets out with COVID to begin the tournament, Rodri stepped into the starting lineup. Rodri played well, controlling the possession crucial to Spain's system. However, Spain was held to draws against Sweden and Poland. Busquets returned for the third game against Slovakia, and Rodri went to the bench. Spain dominated, winning 5–0 and advancing into the knockouts against Croatia. Throughout the knockouts, Rodri served as an energy replacement, shielding tired defenders to close out matches. Spain beat Croatia 5–3 and went to penalty kicks against Switzerland in the quarterfinals. Rodri took Spain's third penalty, which was saved, but his teammates converted theirs to scrape by into the semifinals against Italy. The game again went to penalties, but this time fortune favored the Italians. Rodri wasn't chosen to take a penalty. Still, he proved that he could replace the legendary Busquets in the future.

The 2021–22 season was Rodri's most productive to date. Guardiola reversed his decision from the UCL final, playing Rodri in nearly every match. The year didn't start great for City, with a 1–0 upset in the FA

Community Shield by Leicester City. Disappointment continued in City's various cup endeavors, with the team failing to reach any finals. The UCL exit was most upsetting, as City failed to live up to the new expectations. An unbelievable comeback from Real Madrid in the semifinals sent Rodri's City packing.

But the season wasn't all doom and gloom. With his national team, Rodri saw increased playing time as Spain finished as 2021 Nations League runners-up. The EPL campaign was one of England's greatest title fights between heavyweights City and Liverpool, coming down to the final day, with Rodri leaving his imprint on much of it. Against Everton in November, Rodri scored the Premier League Goal of the Month with a screamer from 20-plus yards. But whatever City did, Liverpool kept pace. Every point was important. On New Year's Day against

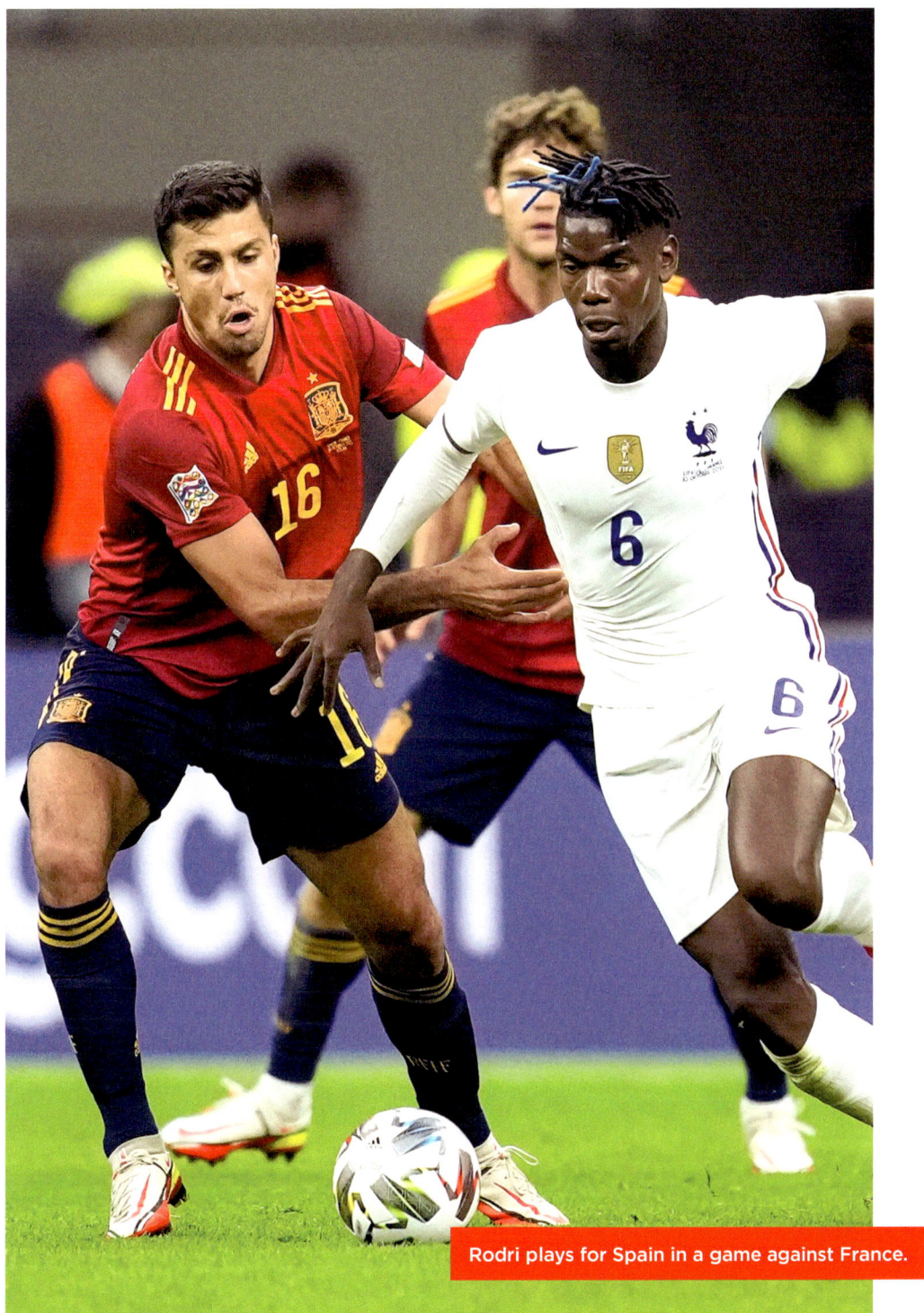

Rodri plays for Spain in a game against France.

Crushing Champions League Exit

City's exit from the 2021-22 Champions League was the season's most painful moment. After a dominant group stage, a round of 16 smashing of Sporting CP, and a feisty 1-0 aggregate win over Rodri's former club Atlético Madrid, Manchester booked a semifinal spot against Real Madrid. The first leg was an entertaining 4-3 win for Rodri and friends. But in the second leg, City suffered an unthinkable loss. With City up 1-0 heading to injury time, Madrid's Rodrygo scored two late goals to send the tie to extra time where Madrid scored another. Rodri stood with head in hands as his same-named opponent was responsible for his dramatic exit.

Arsenal, with the match tied in extra time, Rodri poked a bouncing ball past Aaron Ramsdale to give City three points. The goal kept a 12-match winning streak alive for City, pulling them just ahead of Liverpool.

Rodri closed the season with a barrage of goals. In late April, he tallied in three consecutive matches. With two games remaining, City held a narrow three-point lead in the table. Against West Ham, City trailed 2–0 at half but escaped with a massive draw. Rarely facing a deficit, City had come back from two goals down in

"THREE GOALS IN FIVE MINUTES. HEARTBREAK FOR LIVERPOOL, GLORY FOR MANCHESTER CITY."

the league for the first time since 2012. Liverpool took advantage, winning against Southampton. Heading into the final day, the gap was one point.

Standing between Rodri and the title was 14th-placed Aston Villa. But just like the previous week, Manchester started poorly. Panic crept in as Villa stunned City to go up 2–0. Advantage Liverpool. Needing a hero, up stepped two unlikely scoring threats, Gündoğan and Rodri. A 76th-minute back-post Gündoğan header brought life back to the Etihad. Minutes later, Rodri tied things, scoring one of his classic outside-of-the-box goals. The frenetic City attack hounded over the broken Villa backline and pounced a minute later. Gündoğan scored a tap-in, completing the comeback. Three goals in five minutes. Heartbreak for Liverpool, glory for Manchester City. They were the champions of England by a single point.

Rodri finished his best campaign with seven goals and two assists. Rodri also dominated in passing statistics, leading all midfielders in completions and successful percentage. For his excellent season, on July 12, Rodri extended his City contract until 2027. The team loved him, and Rodri wanted to reach new heights.

RODRI

Atop the Soccer World

City were confident they had the momentum for another massive year. In the Community Shield, Liverpool got the better of Rodri's club, winning 3–1. However, rather than a title fight with Liverpool, Arsenal threatened City's fifth league trophy in six seasons. Arsenal lost just once in their first 19 matches, topping the table early.

OPPOSITE: Rodri celebrates on the pitch during a Manchester City match.

OPPOSITE Rodri (left) and Sergio Busquets (center) battle for the ball with Youssef En-Nesyri of Morocco during a 2022 FIFA World Cup match.

Then came the midseason 2022 FIFA World Cup. With Busquets still performing for the national team, Rodri was creatively utilized as a center back. Rodri's stable presence and passing ability translated to the backline, and he looked comfortable. Spain started the tournament winning 7–0 against Costa Rica, but that was the only win. Spain drew Germany 1–1 and fell to Japan 1–2. Spain narrowly advanced out of the group and were matched up with Morocco. However, Spain was sent home, losing in penalties, as they missed all three of their attempts. Regardless, Rodri showed his versatility and, with Busquets' international retirement, became the first choice CDM.

Returning to Manchester, Rodri locked in for a title fight. Both City and Arsenal rarely dropped points. The matches against each other ultimately determined the

Rodri helped Manchester City win Premier League and UCL trophies.

final outcome. In the first, Rodri helped City dominate the midfield, making four interceptions and seven ball recoveries in a 3–1 win. In the other fixture, City showed their experience, winning 4–1. The wins came during a 16-match unbeaten streak. Rodri helped City secure another league title, finishing with two goals and six assists. The consistent performer was named in the Professional Footballers' Association (PFA) Team of the Year, alongside four of his teammates. Rodri added another domestic trophy in the **FA Cup** with a 2–1 victory in an all-Manchester final.

But the real prize came in the Champions League. City was unbeaten in the group, scoring 14 goals and conceding 2. Rodri allowed only one goal while on the pitch. In the knockouts, Rodri played all but 26 minutes. In the round of 16, City tore apart RB Leipzig, winning

8–1 on aggregate. In the quarterfinals against Bayern Munich, City won 4–1 on aggregate, and Rodri tallied his first UCL goal, unleashing a weak-footed curler into the top left corner. After a 1–1 draw in the first leg of the semis against Real Madrid, Manchester got their revenge in the second. City picked Real apart, decimating them 4–0. Rodri returned to the UCL final hoping for a good outcome. With the EPL and FA Cup trophies secured, the only thing in the way of a **treble** was Inter Milan. After a scoreless first half, City got their goal in the 68th minute. Rodri scored the biggest goal of his career, wrapping a loose ball around a pair of defenders, past André Onana. The kid released in his academy days won City their first Champions League. When the final whistle blew, Rodri fell to his knees in celebration. Rodri was named Man of the Match and Champions League Player of the Season.

Weeks later, Rodri helped guide Spain to a Nations League title, winning against Croatia on penalties. Rodri converted his kick and lifted another trophy. He was again named Player of the Tournament. It was rare for a defensive midfielder to win major awards, but Rodri was that influential.

Rodri lifts the Premier League title trophy.

Rodri came into the 2023–24 season widely recognized as the best defensive midfielder in soccer. In October, Rodri finished fifth in the **Ballon d'Or**. The season also demonstrated just how important he was to City. City competed in seven competitions with a massive trophy haul up for grabs.

First was the Community Shield where Rodri's penalty ghosts came back to haunt him. He missed his kick while Arsenal made theirs. But weeks later, in the UEFA Super Cup, penalty kicks went much better for City as they beat Sevilla. City were eliminated in their first EFL Cup game, as Newcastle snuck by an inexperienced City side 1–0. Rodri featured sparingly in the FA Cup, as his team made a run to the final. In the final, City battled rivals Man United and were defeated 2–1. The loss ended Rodri's streak of 74 straight club appearances without a

Rodri featured strongly in City's key matches in the 2020s.

Best Club

For winning the 2022–23 Champions League, City qualified for the late December FIFA **Club World Cup**. Representing Europe, City played Asian champs Urawa Red Diamonds of Japan in the semifinals. City asserted their dominance in a 3-0 win, with Rodri completing a whopping 108 passes at a 97-percent rate. Rodri was awarded Man of the Match. In the final against South American champion Fluminense of Brazil, Rodri again excelled. In a 4-0 victory, Rodri completed 95 percent of his passes, earning yet another new piece of hardware at age 27. He also won the Golden Ball as the tournament's best player.

defeat. City would collect the FIFA Club World Cup trophy, beating Brazil's Fluminense 4–0.

Entering the UCL as defending champs was a lot of pressure, but the group stage was smooth sailing. City won all six group games. Rodri scored his only goal against Red Star Belgrade. After getting past Copenhagen with a pair of 3–1 wins, City met familiar foes Real Madrid in the quarters. A hectic first leg finished in a 3–3 draw. The second was another classic Madrid–Manchester clash. Real advanced on penalties, eventually winning the title.

City and Arsenal again engaged in a back-and-forth EPL fight. Rodri started the season strongly, scoring in Matchweeks 1 and 3. The latter was an 88th-minute game-winning rocket to win at Sheffield United. City were flying until the game against Nottingham Forest. Leading 2–0, Rodri got in a tussle with Morgan

Gibbs-White, receiving a straight red card for violent conduct. While they escaped the Forest match, City would lose the three matches Rodri was suspended. Arsenal took advantage, leapfrogging them in the table.

Eventually, City came alive. Rodri was instrumental, hitting career highs in goals and assists. A classic Rodri rocket rescued a point against Chelsea. With one game remaining, City led Arsenal by two points. City hosted West Ham in front of an eager Etihad. After a 2–1 first half, Rodri had his big game moment in the 59th minute, restoring the two-goal cushion. City coasted the rest of the match, crushing Arsenal's spirits and becoming the first team to win four consecutive league titles.

Rodri also had a productive international season. In a friendly against Brazil on March 26, Rodri captained Spain and scored the first brace of his career. He was also at the helm of the Spain team that breezed through the 2024 Euros. Rodri had a fantastic tournament, winning Player of the Tournament despite getting injured in the final.

Incredibly, Rodri lost just one of the games he played in for club and country across the year, the FA Cup final. He scored 12 goals, registered 15 assists, and lifted 4 team trophies in 2023–24, a staggering number for a defensive midfielder.

Rodri is part of the backbone of a strong Spain national team.

Heading into the 2024–25 season, Rodri was possibly the best player in the world. He looked to add even more trophies to his ever-growing cabinet. However, the season wouldn't last long. Rodri missed the first few games, recovering from his Euros injury. After a few appearances in September, disaster struck in a league match against Arsenal. Rodri collided with Thomas Partey, landing awkwardly. Rodri went down immediately and had to exit. City would draw the match, but that wasn't the worst of their problems. Rodri tore the ACL and meniscus in his right knee, ruling him out for the season. In his absence, City struggled immensely. In November, they suffered their worst stretch since Guardiola became manager, going winless the entire month. City's midfield looked lackluster without Rodri.

Rodri's spirits were lifted in October as he was awarded soccer's crowning individual award, the Ballon d'Or. Rodri narrowly beat Real Madrid's Vinícius Júnior, becoming just the third Spaniard (the first in 64 years) and first City player to win the award. In his acceptance speech, Rodri spoke about his teammates and almost quitting soccer as a teen. The stress of balancing soccer with school and being released by Atlético almost made him walk away. Luckily, his father got him on the right path, and the rest was history.

The story of Rodri is a tale of persistence, consistency, and excellence. A story of never giving up and a tremendous work ethic. Of doing the little things right and the hard things without question. These are the values that led a humble, school-driven boy from Madrid to the top of the soccer world. Having achieved so much already, the sky's the limit for Rodrigo Hernández.